LIFELONG LEARNERS

LIFELONG LEARNERS

The Journey of Education and Self-Improvement

AVERY NIGHTINGALE

Creative Quill Press

CONTENTS

CHAPTER 1

Introduction

The ability to adapt and be updated with the latest in technology will help us to remain relevant in the job market (or in business) in this age of the digital era. Besides acquiring 'soft' skills, we must also develop 'hard' skills to perform the job consistently with substantial accuracy. In the corporate world, managers may wish to explore new ways for companies to support professionals' lifelong education and self-improvement, be it through specific projects, toward a new way to do a job (CI), or the incorporation of diverse ongoing training opportunities.

To stay relevant and competitive, lifelong learning, or engaging in learning and continual skill development beyond formal education, is increasingly becoming a prerequisite for individual employability. According to the Progress of the World's Women (2015-2016) report by the United Nations Development Programme (UNDP), employment growth is increasingly concentrated in jobs that require tertiary education, and even in countries where employment growth remains largely in secondary education jobs, such positions tend to call for more complex skill levels than in the past. As the nature of work changes with the development of new technologies, there seems to be increasing demands in many jobs for communication, teamwork, analytical, and organizational skills—all of which are associated with quality learning, leading to the development of competencies and a life befitting for a lifelong learner.

CHAPTER 2

Importance of Lifelong Learning

In today's society, change is constant. Also, it not only affects every individual but also the entire workplace in which we immerse ourselves every day. As observed in the groups of study, rooted in the politics of school and workplace, "our priority should be the development of open-minded, self-aware, and self-directed intellectual and social beings who know what they know, know how they know it, know what they still need to know, and know the importance of continuous and recursive learning." The evolving nature of technology and research in varying forms will constantly alter what is known about the human body, our health, and subsequent treatment approaches.

In the present age, people must engage in lifelong learning, a process of seeking continuous educational opportunities for personal and professional growth. At the workplace or outside, knowledge is the key to success. Thus, it is essential for everyone to continue learning, whether learning is going well or not. Lifelong learning plays a role in the process of self-improvement as well as curriculum development. Apart from the development of the individual, all the knowledge acquired transforms not only the individual but also the society as a whole. Lifelong learning is a personal commitment. Most importantly, technology and research are constantly changing and evolving what is known about our bodies, health, and rehabilitation.

CHAPTER 3

Benefits of Continuous Education

The early habit of education creates a high probability of success. Psychologically, the students who attended good education until college received encouragement, and the middle-upper class families created confident people. And unfortunately, age discrimination continues today. Employers prefer university graduates. This is not just a matter of knowledge, but also in terms of future planning has appeared in their life. For the individual, this preparation made up to the last dimensions of having a certain purpose in life and being educated is an important factor in determining this goal. Being an educated person, I do not mean just going to school. Education should be continued throughout life, self-improvement should not be forgotten. To be an educated person is to respect every religion, colleagues, environment, beauty, and order. It is an education to be a person who is eager to do their duties properly regardless of the occupation and to do what they are about to do. In this time period, people who will reach the highest level in terms of self-improvement can fulfill the missions charged.

In this fast-moving world, society is changing every day and I believe education is the key. As much as possible, humans adapt to the pace of the changing society using the knowledge bestowed upon them. Now, let me discuss the significant benefits of continuous education. It is harder to go to a business and say you need to learn more, but this quality is needed most today, living in an extremely complex world, which is continuous and rapid. If some kind of learning attitude is not adopted, no product can emerge. The education and improvement that will continue throughout life are of great importance for the continuation of the product outputs to the figure. The person who continues their education has more job security. Because the educated person is supported by the equation as much as their area of expertise, or if they increase the amount of information about their area of expertise. In these days when there are graduates of 1.5 or 2 diploma programs, the density of education continues to increase, thus creating more quality outputs with a framework that is not very open to competition.

Strategies for Effective Self-Improvement

Deciding on some aspect of daily life you want to change is the first step in deliberate practice. Then design a series of activities where you get out of your comfort zone and perform them alone until you achieve excellence at each one. As the authors note, the most effective people at self-improvement "spend many hours each day pushing themselves beyond the domain or activities in which they feel comfortable." It is also important to set specific and measurable goals for your self-improvement. Make sure that they are measurable, achievable, relevant, and time-bound (SMART goals); ones you know when you've achieved them. Finally, think positively about your effortful action, but still make time for reassessment. Such a system can be hierarchically organized in terms of the specificity of goals. You might want to split a general goal of improving your consistency in running a far distance into two more specific plans of increasing your threshold pace in the 1500m and 3000m within a relevant time-frame. Remember the power of individual character strengths and virtues; hope and courage will drive a need for self-improvement.

Traditionally, there are many tried and true strategies for self-improvement. Chief among them is maintaining a "can-do" attitude through perseverance, dedication, effort, and courage. In other words, it's time to stop being a fence-sitter. You need to be self-accountable for your actions to stay motivated to improve and combat procrastination. It's important to recognize that you should not wait for motivation to make a change. Dedication, effort, and perseverance through an ongoing positive feedback loop is what leads to initiative; just keep moving. You may decide to take a systematic approach to your self-improvement, drawing from what some researchers have called the "deliberate practice" model of personal development.

CHAPTER 5

Overcoming Challenges in Lifelong Learning

Challenges of lifelong learning typically fall on the educator rather than the student, with educational institutions and faculties taking the brunt of the responsibility in developing accessible and applicable learning opportunities for students. "Schwaber speaks to the aspect of training and how the educational field can either properly prepare itself for the fluid, dynamic learning opportunities with successes and drawbacks that aren't always on traditional standards or ignore the situation at hand and compromise their results." Focusing on the technology and the possible educational improvements related to technology is key. Problems with the traditional path of learning can lead to identity issues and other social problems. A lifelong learner could often compromise their own defined beliefs and views in the name of self-improvement; at times, that can hinder any present self-constructed growth of the aforementioned individual.

Learning doesn't always come easily. "Challenges are inherent to the learning process," Artino points out. "In medical education, learners face a number of general challenges including the volume of information, inability to attend to things, stress, high stakes, fatigue." When it comes to lifelong learning, though, it's often obstacles the challenge may not always be obvious. "Just being self-aware of the universal challenges of learning is an important step for educational administrators, instructional designers, educators, and, most essential, the learners themselves," he says, explaining that growth mindset is an important aspect of the learning process. "Individuals who believe in the potential to strengthen their intellect with effort tend to embrace challenges, learn from criticism, find lessons and inspiration in others' successes, and persist despite obstacles. The central message of having a growth mindset is that learning is hard and requires practice and persistence; the practice and persistence really matter."

CHAPTER 6

The Role of Technology in Education

Development in educational technology makes students smarter and brings a paradigm shift in learning. While students in the 21st century love technology, their use of it doesn't always go hand-in-hand with the way educators want them to. It's true that writing has become less popular in the digital age as students are more prone to smart content like instant messaging, social media, email, web pages, and other "content-lite" platforms involving shorter texts. In recent years, technology has changed the game for educators as well. Educators are using educational apps to enhance the interactivity of learning, exploring electronics to create an interactive curriculum. Technology is helping educators and students by controlling the resources and activities systematically, showing the way to explore, and facilitating communications, increasing these skills requests and work together effectively. Google Classroom is proving to be a star in this category.

Technology is transforming every industry it touches, and education is no exception. In today's world, learning new things is not limited to the boundaries of schools or educational institutions. We have access to everything at our fingertips, be it professional courses or a hobby we are passionate about. This is all thanks to the immense progress that technology has brought to the world.

CHAPTER 7

Developing a Growth Mindset

One of the best ways to edit the negative thought processes which lead to the decision that skills and abilities are set in stone is to talk to friends, family, mentors, and coaches about what is being learned. The people who will actively support your progress, be able to point out important roles of knowing you can succeed when challenges occur, and understanding the importance of your goals are the ones that want to be key contributors and dialoguers in your life. It's these close ties that let a lifelong learner truly explore their possibilities and focus on positive discussion, injecting a growth mindset into your veins will overflow in personal development in no time.

Making a decision about learning something new has the potential to go one of two ways: individuals can either decide they're ready, willing, and able to succeed or they can decide that they aren't. Carol Dweck, a highly respected psychologist and University of Stanford professor, identified this predictive difference in millions of students and coined the concepts of "fixed" and "growth" mindset. Those with a fixed mindset or belief that they're either born smart or they aren't decide that brains and talents are genetic and fixed at birth would achieve less in their learning goals; but watch just how much more a group of students who are taught that hard work, self-control, and persistence would exceed the fixed mindset group in grades and overall self-improvement.

CHAPTER 8

Setting Personal Learning Goals

In step 2: Summarize your interest in a single area or activity. Review the various options in your head and look for some kind of pattern, use drawing or summarize them on a sheet. For example, if travel, photography, a good book, are of interest to you, you can easily summarize them as aspirations of a lifetime of adventures to travel to various countries. After a while, hiking through the wilderness and embroidering their adventures in visual and written formats. If what you love most are moments of tranquility, a comfortable armchair and an insightful book, you can figure out how these will nourish your soul. Scalars are key to becoming self-aware.

In step 1: Try to look outside your box for a moment. Analyze your surroundings with a different look. In a technology-driven world, there are tools and useful resources, but sometimes goals remain unattainable because of procrastination or the ease of setting them aside. Try writing down at least three goals you would love to accomplish; they can be anything from personal, career-related or interest-based goals. They can take the form of presentations delivered on Sundays, traveling photography, enjoying a book a month, visualizing a completed project such as learning how to play an instrument or reading good material, anything at all that can bring you personal happiness.

Setting your personal learning goals is as easy as 1, 2, 3.

As we mentioned, once you have set social learning goals, such as learning the latest technology, you can set personal learning goals. They can vary from wanting to learn a new programming language, complete a course for pleasure that you never had the opportunity to explore in college, go green and learn about sociology, or expand your reading list. We customize this space for your learning needs.

Full Scope of Personal Learning Goals

CHAPTER 9

Creating a Learning Routine

The first step to creating a learning routine is to tackle your fear; this is potentially the hardest step for many as it takes a large amount of self-awareness. Fear can hold you back in your learning journey, from spending a day at the museum to learning a new skill. Fear can easily lead someone to create an excuse to hold himself or herself back from obtaining an enriching education. Do not let fear hold you back from knowledge, nothing great ever comes from a comfort zone. However, fear is the only thing that you should have a fear of on your journey to become a lifelong learner. Even those who have always wanted to travel around the world often are too afraid to get out of their own comfortable bubble and make constant excuses to stay in familiar territory. Head on to the "land of all fears!" With each win against your fears, you'll grow as an individual, accomplish your goals, and learn about yourself in ways that the timid you never thought possible.

If learning something new every day can seem overwhelming, think of your lifetime commitment to finding a sense of purpose through learning as your own personal educational marathon. In running a marathon, it typically takes a beginner runner between 12-20 weeks to train for the 42.195 kilometer event. Similarly, training yourself into becoming a lifelong learner is not something that happens overnight but takes time and a well-thought plan. Most individuals who genuinely want a healthier lifestyle through physical activity cannot do so without structuring their day around specific exercise habits. In other words, establishing a routine where you can take the time to learn something new every day should be a goal for any lifelong learner.

CHAPTER 10

Building a Support Network

As you venture through the levels of the Two-Tiered Education System or work on any other major personal project, you will come across plenty of obstacles: student burnout, mountains of resources, and a rapidly-changing environment mixing with personal issues. As the stress accumulates, the degree of importance and motivation you have for some subjects may start to wane. However, these are not insurmountable difficulties. Becoming a proactive learner involves finding help in the many supportive tools provided and around the different communities built in our physical and digital worlds. By doing so, you will evolve into a competent student-teacher, with an attractive skill set and the additional benefits of personal refinement and new results.

While you may feel like you are in this alone, you are anything but. There are local organizations, message boards, clubs and groups, as well as online forums and communities centered around learning. The key is to put yourself out there as much as possible. That way, if you sit down and feel like you are not making any progress, you have plenty of people to turn to. Blogging about your journey is a terrific aid. It is even better if you make contact with other established bloggers and contribute to their sites. Writing not only refreshes your memories but also gets you thinking more deeply about the learning process, especially when your "lived" experience gains precedence over old book knowledge. And of course, in any forum, blog, or group, do not only network, but provide some support as well. The more you invest in others, the more you will receive in return.

CHAPTER 11

Exploring Different Learning Methods

The first (and most obvious) cost-effective idea is reading. We are now able to access a multitude of the world's best-selling self-improvement books and guides, all for affordable, competitive prices. The investment in time is the most likely factor here, but we take from these readings as much as we put into the task. Another popular learning method would be attending lectures if we're given that opportunity. While some would argue finding a talented speaker for a talk on a challenging topic is challenging, we at least have the chance to ask thoughtful questions and engage in comments with other attendees for a direct perspective on the subject, and presented by speaking professionals. If you're not big on lectures, then podcasts are for you. Podcasts do take time, and getting through all the podcasts within a regular line-up is a process.

Over the past 5 years, I've become familiar with a variety of different learning styles, from the traditional educator-learner dynamic to self-taught piano and guitar practice. Thanks to technology, the web is ripe with knowledge in the forms of podcasts, infographics, online slides of university courses, and countless video tutorials. That being said, the following options for learning should likely appeal to anyone looking to learn, at any stage, and caters to any kind of investment in time and money.

CHAPTER 12

Enhancing Critical Thinking Skills

This toolkit is the centerpiece of the project and is claimed to be one of the first of its kind available for use in Canadian college teaching. This toolkit contains strategies and resources that can be used in many of the college classrooms, acting as a supplement to other subjects. Faculty can use most of their curriculum information and add critical thinking objectives effectively. The findings from this study suggest a need for colleges to create a more student-centered learning environment. Consideration of models where teachers take the role of facilitator in the classroom and encourage open dialogue, provide guidance, and direct students to educate themselves may provide a more effective way to deliver learning in the 21st century and promote the learning-to-learn process needed to graduate engaged learners and passionate lifelong learners.

Adult learners are much less likely than recent high school graduates to attend full-time and may require scheduling accommodations around work, parenting, and other responsibilities. To remain competitive, colleges and universities are creating innovative programs that accommodate the schedules of learners who may be unable to participate in traditional paths. One research study is discussed, which finds that educational technology, the internet, and user-friendly software can engage learners in active, student-centered learning and provide students and working adults with the opportunity to 'learn how to learn'.

CHAPTER 13

Improving Communication Skills

The importance of setting communication expectations with learners is an important first step to creating a successful educational experience. On the first day of class, a syllabus should be provided that identifies how students can best communicate with the instructor and any established forums, such as chat rooms or discussion boards, that allow for student interactivity. In addition, a philosophy of communication and detailed instructions should be provided for Benjamin Bloom's six types of knowledge, which consist of factual, conceptual, procedural, metacognitive, or strategic knowledge. Finally, establishing a proper reaction should the student prove his knowledge in any of these areas. Email correspondence should be kept professional and any discussions had among learners should be respectful and appropriate. Profanity in any type of communication will not be tolerated, and students are encouraged to see their academic advisor if there are problems communicating with either the instructor or their classmates.

Strong communication skills are essential when it comes to engaging learners and ensuring that content is relatable and relevant. Successful communication skills involve active listening and the creation of a shared understanding, which can contribute to a more rewarding experience for today's lifelong learners. Instructors are more likely to leave a lasting impression on lifelong learners if communication is clear and well-structured. Active listening is key when it comes to understanding learner needs and, in turn, providing the most engaging educational experience possible.

CHAPTER 14

Acquiring New Knowledge and Skills

Education to become a lifelong learner involves the ability to learn from all opportunities presented by daily life. True learning is an activity where the individual not only memorizes data, but also goes through all experience and learning processes. The ability to learn is not affected by place or age. On the contrary, learning is a lifelong process that should be put into practice every day, and there is never an age that is too early or too late to acquire new knowledge, skills, or abilities. Potential difficulties should be seen as motivation to activate the knowledge that the individual already possesses, and to create opportunities to develop the ability to learn new things and improve the skills they already possess.

Education, in the broadest sense of the word, encompasses any activity that helps an individual not only acquire new knowledge and skills, but also develop and improve oneself. It also includes the development of one's critical thinking and self-efficacy, as well as the capacity to face and overcome adversity. The teaching of these abilities in a school environment is not enough, and it is essential that this learning process takes place when individuals are outside of school. Any individual who does not give priority to developing a lifelong learning perspective may be left behind. Immanuel Kant provides us with a piece of advice when he makes the allegory that if an individual does not seek to become better each day, then the day is wasted. True learning is found in the micro-improvements made every day. In short, an individual should strive to be at least 1 percent better every day.

CHAPTER 15

Expanding Cultural Awareness

However, in almost every culture, patterns of formal education and ethics are interlocked and interdependent. Paradoxically, or so it seems, we have posed the question of democracy even though we had not yet adopted an education system based on the idea of a citizen who knows and practices the ground rules and virtues of democracy. Similarly, with all efforts of lifelong learning constituting the lifelong learning trend, paradoxically, it seems, we have been talking about global citizens, illustrating their abilities, virtues, opinions, and practices, but we had yet to put into practice educational systems with the aim of forming these citizens. The final reflection is that the idea of global citizens, despite constituting the final equation of all these elements, is not in the educational systems.

Experiencing and understanding different cultures can help a learner to see and understand the complexities and issues of education systems in these various cultures. For people who have become excited about and have begun lifelong learning in their own cultural arena, transcultural learning as lifelong learners can come to have a profound impact on understanding and appreciating human diversity, as well as the complexity both of educational processes that human societies have developed over centuries and of the issues in education. John Dewey, the famous sociologist and educational philosopher, said, "Education can foster community life, but only if we think of community as including as many varied cultural forms as are represented on the face of the earth."

Nurturing Creativity and Innovation

Contrary to this belief, across developed and developing nations, the educational institutions are observing far from the expected development in creativity and innovations from the adults, and thus, such competitiveness expected from high levels of knowledge and built competences are not being observed. Consequently, "skilled job positions" at various levels continue to be filled by foreigners, impinging on national sovereignty and triggering worries among the local workforce. Often, graduates find themselves taking up traditional jobs and are set on doing boring repetitive work. This deviation from the anticipated outcomes of a continually improving quality of human capital objectives can, in fact, be attributed to an inherent error in the current education system. Common educational systems, all across nations, are collectively designed on assumptions that people are hapless indefinite knowledge vacuums and can be fully and permanently dumped with systematically organized information and skills within the formal school timeframe.

To learn is a lifelong endeavor. We start learning from the moment we are born and stop only when we die. All our life, we acquire knowledge and information and build up skills and faith. Thus, we improve ourselves in every aspect, whether that be intellectual, spiritual, or physical. Traditionally, learning has been closely associated with education.

School is the key driver of resh astem was not so long ago. Under this belief, large and high investments continue to go into formal schooling, and now, as a result, many youth become college or university graduates. There is a common perception that tertiary education is the crucial part of human capital. It is a common thought that through the continuous building of the cognitive and motor skills of them and the knowledge gained, our young will improve their competences until becoming highly skillful and creative adults who innovate on a lifelong basis. Education, in other words, is intended to be this never-ending continuing process for achieving the potential of creativity and innovation in our people.

CHAPTER 17

Adapting to Change and Embracing Uncertainty

One of the greatest difficulties of training in Uncertainty disciplines is that the concepts are hidden from general scrutiny. Only with the development of the calculus do we have the foundation for addressing these problems that have remained dormant for almost a century. Leibniz and Newton, around 1676, were the first to appreciate the value and necessity of self-knowledge as a means to reach the laws of nature. They invented the word Oeconomics. Oikonomia is a very old term of Greek culture with a new meaning, the Science of Sciences. Hesiod of Ascreus in the 8th century before Christ, in the poem "Working and the Days," writes the first manual on Oikonomia addressed to his brother Pitheacous, a righteous simple man ignoring the war activity previous to the political structure of aristocrats' oligarchs in his way to enriching Aristotle 21 centuries later. The collaboration between individuals who want to create something new is impossible without adaptation to change, consequently impossible to exist fixed forms of pedagogical systems. The teacher-inspired role is too unequivocally mystical to support Education. We need Institutions in the context of which we can immerse ourselves freely for an indefinite period of time and gain awareness. Therefore, the institutional liabilities will have to be redefined with a major impact on institutional theory.

What kind of challenges and new changes do we handle? The first question that arises in our mind is regarding the rate, scale, and unceasing nature of change, and the increasing complexity of the decisions that arise from that change. We come across so many barriers within the individual that hinder learning. To survive in this knowledge era, all human beings are learners and have to be continuously. We are here to examine some issues which have a great influence on the individual's lifelong learning. In this interconnected age, embracing ignorance is a form of wisdom. Trading knowledge requires a heavy tax. Imposing simplifications means ruling ignorance. The only real freedom is wisdom. It's time to just blend out of the white noise. The nature of our subject is human ignorance and uncertainty. The principle of uncertainty is deeply connected with all other scientific principles. Therefore, educators, scientists, philosophers, and thinkers must finally work together synergistically to enlighten human ignorance and uncertainty.

CHAPTER 18

Balancing Work, Education, and Personal Life

Some tips to balance work and education include scheduling your time wisely and prioritizing your duties. While your friends might be bar-hopping and eating out, you might have to pass on a Wednesday night dinner and study for your upcoming quiz that's worth 20 percent of your class grade. You might have to study during your lunch break, or even just take a 15-minute walk outside so you don't feel burned out. While it might seem like working and going to school is impossible, trust in yourself and make the necessary sacrifices to accomplish both of your goals. It won't be easy, but it will be rewarding. And while aiming high academically and professionally, don't forget about your personal well-being and your mental health. Upon graduation, you'll look back at this chapter of your life and realize that it was the ultimate test of self-reliance, time management and maturity. It might seem like a balancing act, especially when everything around you starts tipping. But remember: those who believe in you expect you to succeed, and your journey is just around the corner. So patience is your best friend, and it's okay to take things day-by-day while working toward your dreams.

You're finally in the groove of handling your coursework and not having to worry about work. But that sense of relief might only last for a few months. Once autumn rolls around, you might find yourself juggling a full-time job, your college or graduate school classes, and making time for yourself and your personal life. Sound daunting? You're not alone. Many working graduate and undergraduate students have to balance their time and energy to accommodate their academic efforts and personal commitments. Some students will have to make time to help take care of kids, tend to aging parents, or other family-related duties. Luckily, your hard work and dedication won't go unnoticed, and in the end, you're going to come out of this period of your life stronger than when you entered it.

CHAPTER 19

Overcoming Procrastination and Time Management

Another simple idea to beat procrastination is to do things bit by bit instead of all in one go. For example, breaking a wide project into smaller tasks and arranging your deadlines can be equally manageable and successful. Psychiatrist David Burns also advises time-based conclusions: dedicate at least ten minutes to doing whatever it is that you procrastinate. The prospect of working on something tedious for ten minutes (manageable) instead of all afternoon (stressful) is manageable indeed! Problematically, procrastination and time-wasting form an almost symbiotic relationship. When you are procrastinating you waste time, and when you are wasting time, you might as well procrastinate. But time-wasting and procrastination are not the same thing. While procrastination is putting off something important, time-wasting is aimless and harmless – one can waste time browsing through books in a library or strolling about in the sunshine and nature – it still counts as a positive use of time. Time-wasting can of course turn into procrastination if it eats up time; however, activities which are not of worth are more likely to lead to constructive pursuits than procrastination does.

Some things to help win the procrastination war are deceptively obvious. One of these is doing something. People usually procrastinate because they do not want to do something, thinking that once begun, it will put you under pressure to complete; pressure which as a result, will make the task more difficult and stressful. However, by doing something, an individual takes the task from the realm of wishful thinking and imagination into the realm of reality. In short, the person takes one crucial step towards getting things done. Also, doing anything often opens the door toward another, not only energizing an individual to complete more but also potentially leading towards a different accomplishment entirely. Procrastinators often find themselves doing something else when procrastinating anyway, so it helps to at least aim that doing something is actually productive.

CHAPTER 20

Utilizing Resources for Lifelong Learning

Through this program, a dedicated team and professional curriculum developers are available as representatives of regularly integrated third-party companies. Also, we can certainly contribute creatively by sharing our experiences, expertise, experience, and knowledge so that the content developed in this program is relevant, enjoyable and useful in various ways in various contexts. Nowadays we are proud to work with many researchers, professionals and experts in many areas, as well as implement integrated interdisciplinary approaches. That will help us make our learning program not only more interesting and effective, but also help build a supportive multi-faceted community of learners who have a common goal to be lifelong learners who are continuously improving. Our collaboration proved to have created a wide concept of learning quality from one stage to another.

The term education refers to an experience involving learning, growth, and improvement. Education is a living, lifelong journey, and as learning beings, we are perpetual students and teachers. However, the foundation of what we often perceive as education is a human invention "that has long since been adopted by patterns of inherited and maturation." This subject has drawn worldwide attention since ancient times to this day and over time education has improved so much and developed into various forms according to various needs. In school or campus, we will learn how to collect and implement relevant and useful knowledge. This valuable knowledge and information must be searched wisely because the value of information will be increasingly exploited through the accumulation of useful knowledge.

CHAPTER 21

Engaging in Continuous Professional Development

The Federal Technology Transfer Act [FTTA] of 1986 added section 211 c. to the original 1980 Stevenson-Wydler Act (SWA), setting forth the basic training responsibilities of federal technology transfer agency personnel. Pursuant to that section, the US Congress in 1987 codified universal training standards and set one year as the minimum tenure for all technology transfer specialists. Network Resource Inc. prepared government-wide technology transfer knowledge and skill standards aligned with the federal budget system. During the Clinton Administration, a newly-created technology transfer Council reported an average of 60% of departmental budgets spent on on-the-job learning, impressive evidence for the vitality of the so-called tech transfer revolution that had taken place in numerous departments and agencies. At Desert Research Institute, a technical training assignment program was in place which required employees to upgrade 10 skills for an applied science career path within 10 years of their start date.

Public service employees are expected to engage in continuous learning and professional development. Pertinent US statutes include the General Schedule Leader Grade Evaluation Guide on lifelong learning as well as Under 5 U.S.C. subsection 4111, paragraph 8, which reports to Congress each year on the amount and type of training offered during the then past fiscal year. Additionally, under 5 U.S.C. subsection 4103, there is a general requirement that all federal employees receive (as well as the duty of all employees to avail themselves of) training or development "designed to improve the performance of current duties or performance in preparation for, or in support of, career development into the highest level job and pay of the employee's career, as well as mission accomplishment and organizational goal achievement." Many agencies have been working with an HR University Special Interest Group since the start of the Administration to identify various profession model standards and agency career paths.

CHAPTER 22

Pursuing Higher Education and Formal Degrees

Conceivably, the student "tour" of higher education, traditional or unconventional, constitutes a form of "bricoleur" loosely picking and joining "bits and pieces" of educational, developmental, and academic experience that, when combined, create a desirable educational outcome or product. A departure from a rather less formative period of employment to another. Yet if this is taken to be so, just which bits and pieces of that higher-level educational experience or academic study represent the fragments, and from what is the planning or making of this academic outcome or study? Instructional designers routinely emphasize the "whole," not just "bits and pieces." Consequently, the learner's journey must take account of curricular or degree planning or show the evidence of students having followed some formal plan. To form the beginning of an answer to that question, I would like to consider a later manifesto implemented at the level of educational curriculum.

It should come as no surprise, given the range of students in higher education today, to be informed that many mature students, even those attending full-time courses, may have family or work responsibilities. But they too can benefit from undergraduate study. This higher educational "tourism", exhibited by mature students who perhaps might study an undergraduate degree part-time alongside full-time dedicated "day student" employment, may invariably prepare them for lifelong learning and readiness for the demands of the 21st-century globalized knowledge economy. They additionally bring both fresh perspectives and extensive life experiences to a cohort of conventional day students. Most obviously, mature students are at a distinct advantage if they are studying as a means of genuine self-development.

CHAPTER 23

Exploring Online Learning Platforms

The education sector exploits technology advancement to make their jobs easier, including the teacher. The development is none other than to make learning more optimal and efficient by utilizing technology services. So many different learning platforms are now more recognized. Unfortunately, in the end, most technology-based students are only students on social media and YouTube. They think this can be used as a tool to learn. In fact, there are still many educational online platforms that can be used to get everybody's education quickly, cheaply, and easily. There are a lot of platforms or websites like Duolingo, Khan Academy, Coursera, EdX, Udemy, Udacity, Lynda, Codecademy, LinkedIn Learning, YouTube, podcasts, other blogs, and still many others (Azani, 2019).

In the 21st century, when people need to find information on a specific inquiry, they always Google it. Instead of passively visiting a website, people use technology to actively learn and apply the knowledge to their lives. A baby scientist, Sal (2006), who thought the same way, launched his own educational YouTube Channel (The Khan Academy) to teach people mathematics and science. That's how we learn in the United States, and not just us, the people from all over the world (Burnett, 2010, p. 26). As known, in today's technology era, most things are done by using devices and the internet. Technology has changed the way people learn, which is responsible for entertainment before. Despite the advancement of technology, so many people think that understanding everything about technology and the usage of devices make them enough to empower themselves completely without any need for education and study. This results in a lack of seriousness in learning.

CHAPTER 24

Participating in Workshops and Training Programs

I've had some really good time going to illustration workshops where the teacher would come to my table and leave some tips that would fix the illustration. It was something essential I needed as I had hit a plateau. You can gain more knowledge by training, listening, and doing. By being consistent in practicing and collaborating with different artists, I ended up building a strong portfolio, which helped me get my first project in a big agency. Even though art is not a sprint race, I've learned that you have to be consistent so that people have you in mind by the end of the marathon. Then, when a marathon is happening, you end up getting invited. I like running metaphors, sorry!

If you're interested in a specific field, doing everything it takes to become better at it pays off. Participating in workshops and training programs provides opportunities to learn and understand the know-how in the field. It's also a great way to meet like-minded people and industry professionals, sharing the experience and knowledge. Most of the workshops are usually held by someone who is educated and has a lot of experience, who will be sharing their story, the ins and outs of the industry, and how to tackle the challenges one may face. When I go to a workshop, I'm always prepared for the real OGs to share some truth and wake people up.

CHAPTER 25

Joining Learning Communities and Discussion Groups

One other nerve-wracking task is joining learning communities. Joining a learning community is similar to joining in a discussion group, but people who frequently gather in learning communities all have one purpose; they are all interested in the same field of study. Learning communities can be the perfect place for people who are interested in having a deeper conversation and in expanding their skills with others. The last thing you want to keep in mind is that when you start frequenting these communities, many people will have the opportunity to see your personality and character. In the modern era, our lives are dramatically changed within a flash of a second. To keep up and adapt to all the changes, continuously raising one's own awareness and self-improvement is essential. As you stroll on the illustrious journey of your education and self-improvement, people's envy could potentially change into an influence toward them wanting to be much like yourself!

We all have ideas, perspectives, and views that we would like to share with others, and you probably have that same kind of feeling inside of you. For example, the idea of having a savings account, the latest products that you've tried recently, or that hangout place that was incredibly exciting. Not only sharing your thoughts will increase our self-esteem, confidence, and self-image, but it is also much fun to share what we have just learned with people who share similar interests. You may also feel the same to learn some new things and gain new ideas through others. Speak up your thoughts and act now. It's time to join a discussion group or a learning team!

CHAPTER 26

Seeking Mentorship and Guidance

In The Juilliard School's Alumni Magazine from the mid-90s, there is an article that discusses various alumni and sharing their thoughts on the necessity of mentorship. Violinist Itzhak Perlman elaborates on the concept of teaching versus guiding a pupil, stating, "You don't only show them how to play the violin, you have to make sure that they have some sort of life after that. A musician has to have everything else in life, too." Mentorship is key for individuals embarking upon the diverse path of a young, hungry student ready to take their first bite and serve as an invaluable resource as they grow. Thought to be Everett's magnum opus, Josh and Company in the Land of Ever: The Next Level follows three of the series' previous mentees who have been raised to a mentorship role within a sequence known as Second Level. Having been given the task of learning a complicated concept with no clear guidelines, each takes a unique approach to the task, and a great deal of oneself is learned through the action.

Mentorship is an invaluable resource for individuals at any stage in life, exposing young learners to a world of possibilities and connecting them with an experienced source of guidance and support. Quite simply, a mentor, as defined by Merriam-Webster, is a trusted counselor or guide. This commonly older, more knowledgeable individual is capable of providing similar assistance to the teacher, being able to serve as an invaluable tool for those looking to navigate an unfamiliar path, offering resources and aid that are often necessary to successfully land a position within that field.

CHAPTER 27

Reflecting on Learning Experiences

All reflective exercises are not created equally, be they blind inquisitions in the personal journal of the transitioning student or intellectually transparent laboratory experiments in the classroom. Ideally, a reflective experience is capable of producing transformative changes that encourage students to write stories rather than posts and to forge communities, not countries. Only by doing so can students appreciate the significance of the presidential quote that Dr. Mary Deane Sorcinelli, University of Massachusetts-Amherst, saved for the conclusion of her powerful keynote. Sorcinelli quotes John Quincy Adams, sixth president of the United States, who once said, "In the end, it's not about the curriculum. It's the relationships that matter."

As lifelong learners reflect on the learning experiences, they create a mental road map inspired by triumphs and failures. Reflective writers may record the most significant classroom moments in a simple journal or compare day one to week four, and later week eight, in a project. Reflective learners take seriously the idea of "fool me once, shame on you; fool me twice, shame on me." Rarely, if ever, will reflective learners fall for the same trick. Reflective learners may never smooth out self-imposed peaks and valleys but, instead, coast on a perpetual upward trajectory. While reflective learners may plateau, they will never slip. Ultimately, biochemist Bard Urbassik characterizes deep-rooted reflective learning with the adage, "make failure your teacher, not your undertaker."

CHAPTER 28

Evaluating and Measuring Learning Progress

Learning, or the acquisition of pre-planned knowledge and skills, may be defined as the compiling, organizing, and delivering of new cognitive or motoric 'assets' and accompanying neural representations over some time t, often in a graded manner, whether gradually, step-by-step, or in token or increments or a 'question by question' manner. In the traditional learning 'crescendo' model commonly employed in our educational systems worldwide, the developed cognitive or motoric assets, at 1 year after learning was introduced, may be operationally referred to as '1.0 year learning skill score'. Cognitive or motoric assets are known to 'fade' or cause learning degradation due to exposure to noncomprehension of non-applied knowledge or skills. This work addresses learning progress that is 'sustained after initial learning maintenance efforts' and attempts 'to avoid triggering of adversative knowledge or skill fading'.

A good education venture should be properly quantified for its efficiency, effectiveness, and in some cases, for its success. This article encapsulates key concepts in measuring learning progress in different stages of a human lifespan, beginning from early childhood during the pre-K years through the completion of a formal degree or when lifelong self-improvement undergoes a sudden halt. Evaluation of learning takes place at the individual student or group of students, or instruction/

educational intervention levels, with aims comparable to healthcare, of identifying solutions to problems in a timely manner. The comprehensive developmental and learning progress system proposed in this article was recently provided in Shapiro et al., a work voted Best Paper in the Pre-K to Grade 12 Educational Evaluation Section, American Evaluation Association, 2006.

CHAPTER 29

Celebrating Achievements and Milestones

This is a film project but it is also linked to my reading goal since I am inspired by various tales of the unknown. I realize this is just my second film under my second Kickstarter campaign but I promise it will be worth your "donation". If you care to check out my first campaign, here's the link. The majority of the people who backed me that first go round will get everything for free for their generosity. Of course, don't forget, I have felt your help through my journey. It is now up to me to continue on and share my art. And WOW!! Thank you for all the support!!! Thank you for following along. It's your incentive that is driving me forever to be a lifelong learner.

Another journal day! In the next step, 10 days after my last journaling, I mentioned the mini projects and anniversaries I might celebrate. I just began writing the script for "Speaking In Tongues: The Man Who Lived Again". While I am not sure if Ebullio would call that a "miniproject", it is certainly milestone worthy. The script is only a couple pages long. It felt great to write those out! I am doing my best not to rush. Unlike past film scripts, this one is not about using the visuals but rather the dialogue and other audio elements. Aside from being my homage to the classic Twilight Zone tales, it is also a reference to the episodes that showcase memorable voice work. Reflecting on these great pieces of entertainment, penning my own "Golden Age of Radio"-esque thriller puts a smile upon my face.

CHAPTER 30

Inspiring Others to Embrace Lifelong Learning

Use social media as an integrated lifelong learning experience. Access the entire world of people who know more things than you. This means joining team discussions to collaborate. With apps like Twitter, LinkedIn and other professional outlets, get involved. Do not worry whether you look good and feel horribly uncomfortable starting, to be nice. Sharing a nice tale doesn't make you subject matter. The point is, how can all of us associate, build networks and explore fresh concepts together and utilize resources.

There are moments in one's life in which people who are passionate about learning something are working on something which is ground-breaking and innovative. You need to find these moments for yourself and for them. Just interesting people with interesting ideas will live surrounded by a forest of "light bulb" moments. These calls are moments of revelation, when you see a situation upside-down, and your sight comes to be like the light. You need to reach those states of mind throughout your lifelong learning process and find these moments not only for yourself, but also for those around you. You are on a lifelong journey of learning, and should be surrounded by those who enjoy encouraging, lifting and propelling you to greatness (and vice versa). Remember, you are the average of the five people you associate with most, and that is why other people will support you in learning videos, sharing stories about articles and learning from mistakes, in addition to helping challenge and cultivate you. As Sir Richard Steele was quoted as saying, "Reading is in the mind of the mind, the latter in discourse, and exercises both of them".

CHAPTER 31

Conclusion

Lifelong learners are neither the result of improvisation nor a promise made by a salesman. They are the philosophy of a man whose lifelong learning perspective has been fortunate to be seen in action. Lifelong learners embrace their essence through wisdom, transparency, and continuous curiosity. Among many scenarios, being a lifelong learner today makes the "new normal": learning neither static nor imposed, but an action of leaders to develop skills, with an essential change because lifelong learners consider that "normal" will never be the same as it was. The lifelong learner is an autodidact who knows that the opportunities for learning not only come from books or academic successes but internalize all possibilities of life experiences, recognizing as valid not only the achievements, but also the least of the failures, because in them, and in reflection, the greatest values are learned.

2020 has had to face significant challenges; nonetheless, it is our individual responsibility to become better versions of ourselves. Influenced by new technologies and new generations, lifelong learners will examine their progress individually and could even include the essential characteristics of millennials and the new generations: transparency, wisdom, curiosity, courage, flexibility, empathy, open-mindedness, leadership, responsibility, and a totally humanized self. Under these parameters, should there be a substantial redefinition of the educational content, in the light of the Darwinian thesis, "Evolve or die," and that today resounding the author of "Microsoft" manifesting "Nobody will be ahead if they do not continue learning?"